My First Joke Book

for Kids Ages 3-6

Laugh out Loud with Silly One Liners, Would

You Rather Questions, Hilarious Knock-Knocks, and Tongue Twisters

Brooke Keller

ISBN: 9798484975136 (Paperback)
ASIN: B09HVXQC6R (Ebook)

Illustrations by Genesis Gelbes

First printing edition 2021.

WHY DID THE BANANA GO TO THE DOCTOR?

BECAUSE IT WASN'T PEELING WELL.

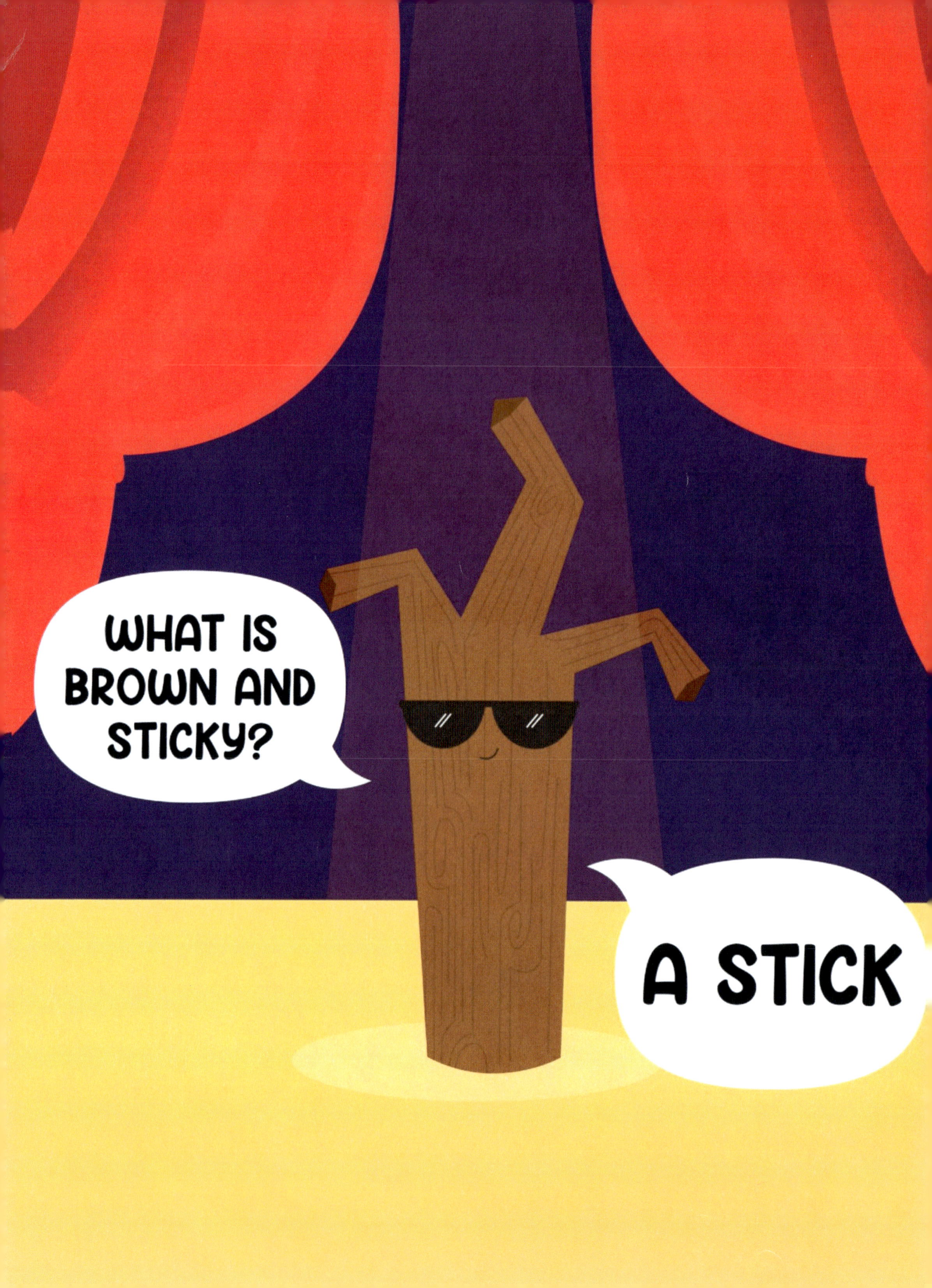
WHAT IS BROWN AND STICKY?
A STICK

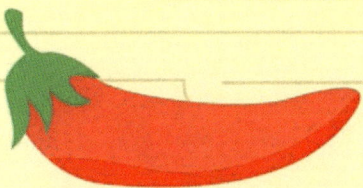

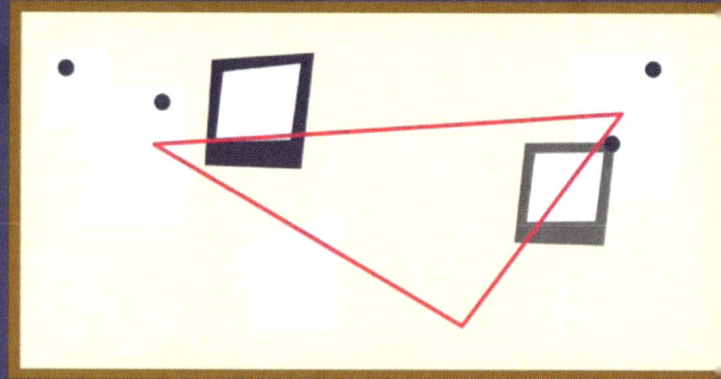

WHAT DO YOU CALL A FAKE NOODLE?

AN IMPASTA

WHAT DO YOU CALL
TWO BIRDS IN LOVE?

TWEET HEARTS

HOW DO YOU MAKE
AN OCTOPUS LAUGH?

WITH TEN-TICKLES.

WHAT DO YOU CALL A SLEEPING BULL?

A BULL-DOZER!

WHY IS 6 AFRAID OF 7?
BECAUSE 7 8 9

WHY DID THE DUCK CROSS THE ROAD? BECAUSE IT THOUGHT IT WAS A CHICKEN

WHY DIDN'T THE ZOMBIE
CROSS THE ROAD?
HE DIDN'T HAVE THE GUTS.

WHY DID THE COW
CROSS THE ROAD?
SO HE COULD
GO THE MOO-VIES!

WHY DID THE CHEWING GUM CROSS THE ROAD? IT WAS STUCK TO THE CHICKEN'S FOOT.

WHAT KIND OF TREE FITS IN YOUR HAND?

A PALM TREE

WOULD YOU RATHER ONLY BE ABLE TO GET AROUND BY BOUNCING LIKE A KANGAROO

OR LEAPING LIKE A BALLERINA?

WOULD YOU RATHER
WAKE UP WITH A SQUIRREL
TAIL OR A RABBIT'S NOSE?

WOULD YOU RATHER HAVE TO WEAR A CLOWN WIG OR A CLOWN NOSE FOR THE REST OF YOUR LIFE?

KNOCK, KNOCK.

WHO'S THERE?
NEEDLE.
NEEDLE WHO?

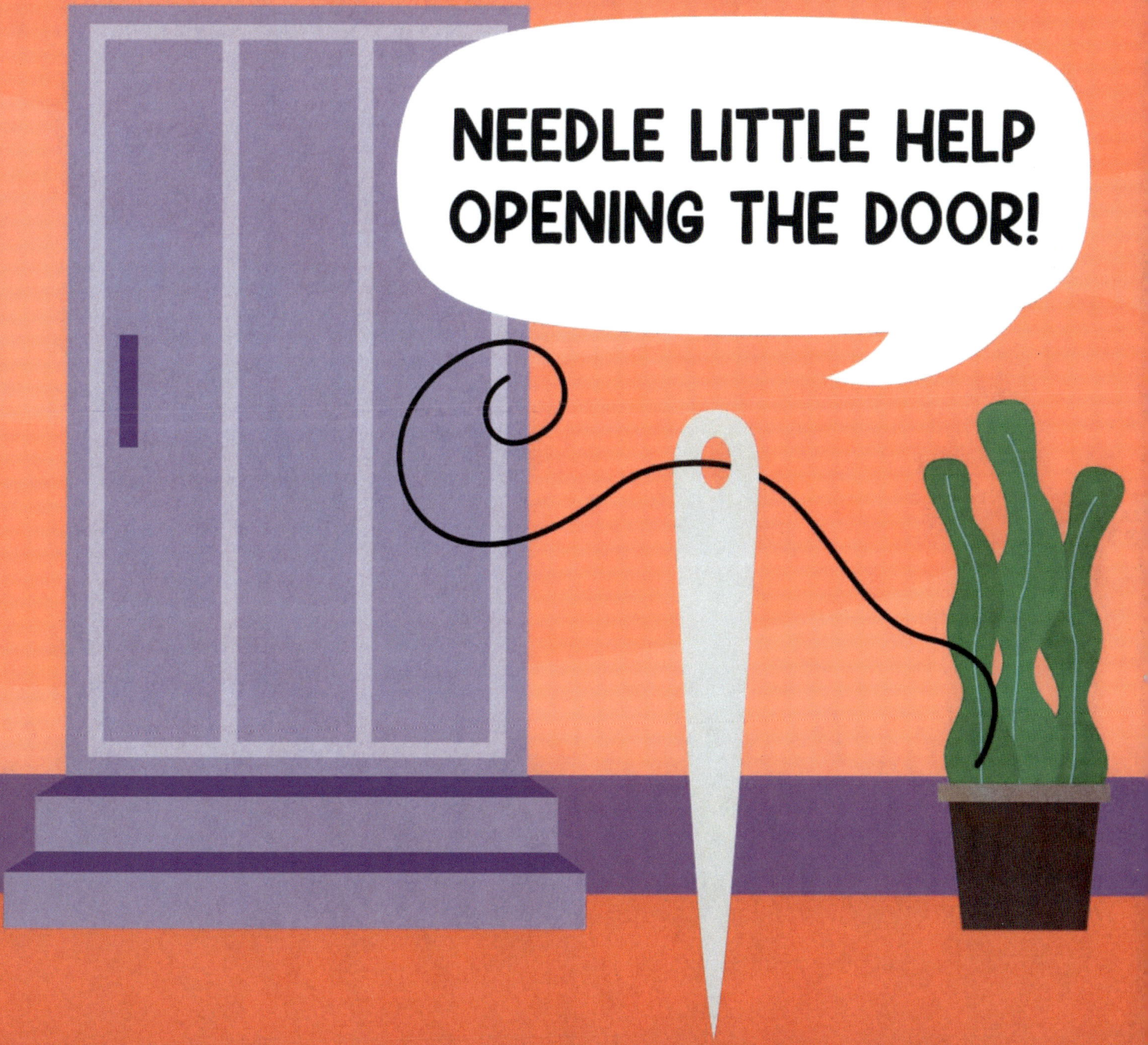

KNOCK, KNOCK.

WHO'S THERE?

HOWL.

HOWL WHO?

HOWL YOU KNOW UNLESS
YOU OPEN THE DOOR?

KNOCK, KNOCK

WHO'S THERE?
COWS GO.
COWS GO WHO?

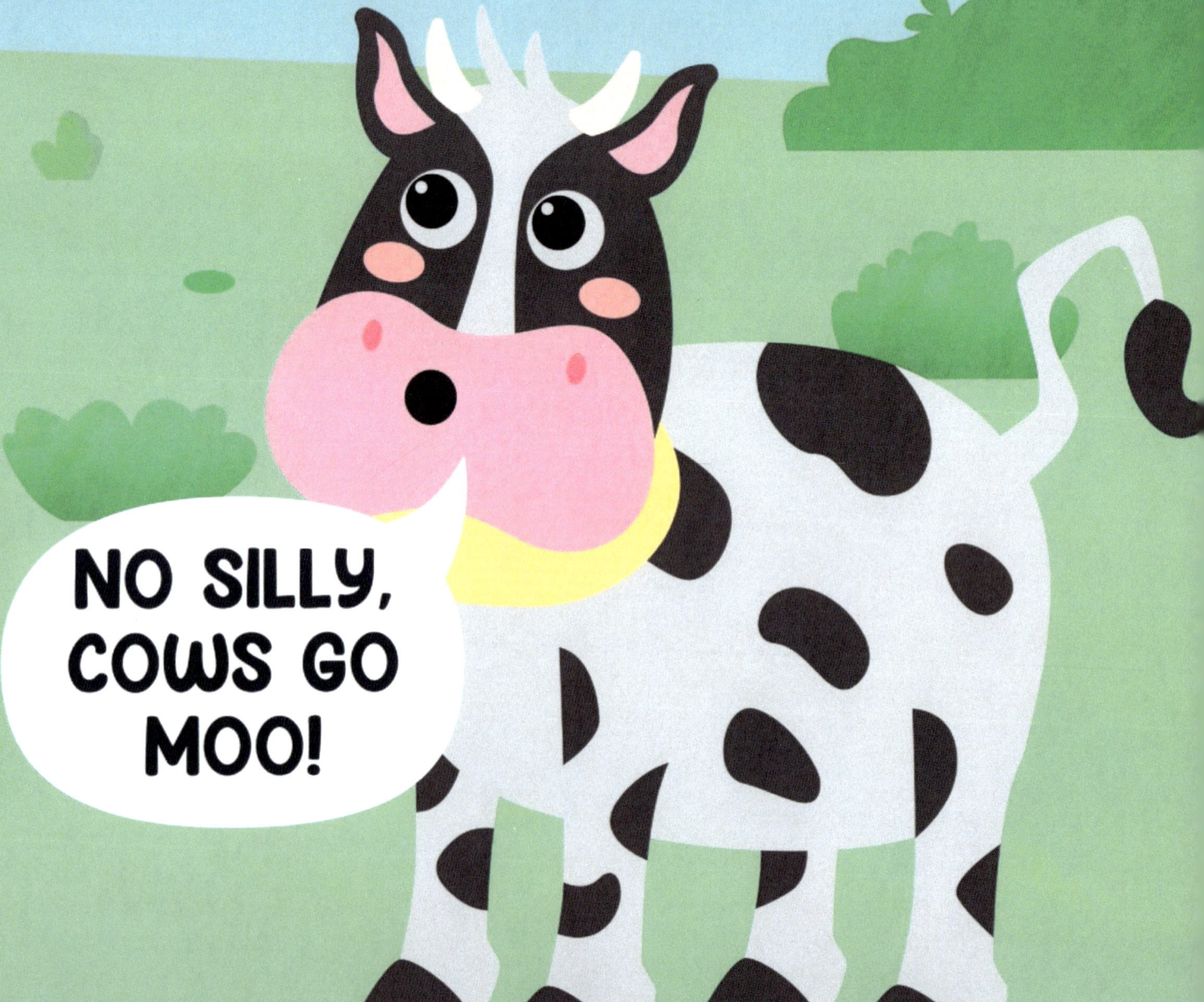

KNOCK, KNOCK.

WHO'S THERE?

KANGA.

KANGA WHO?

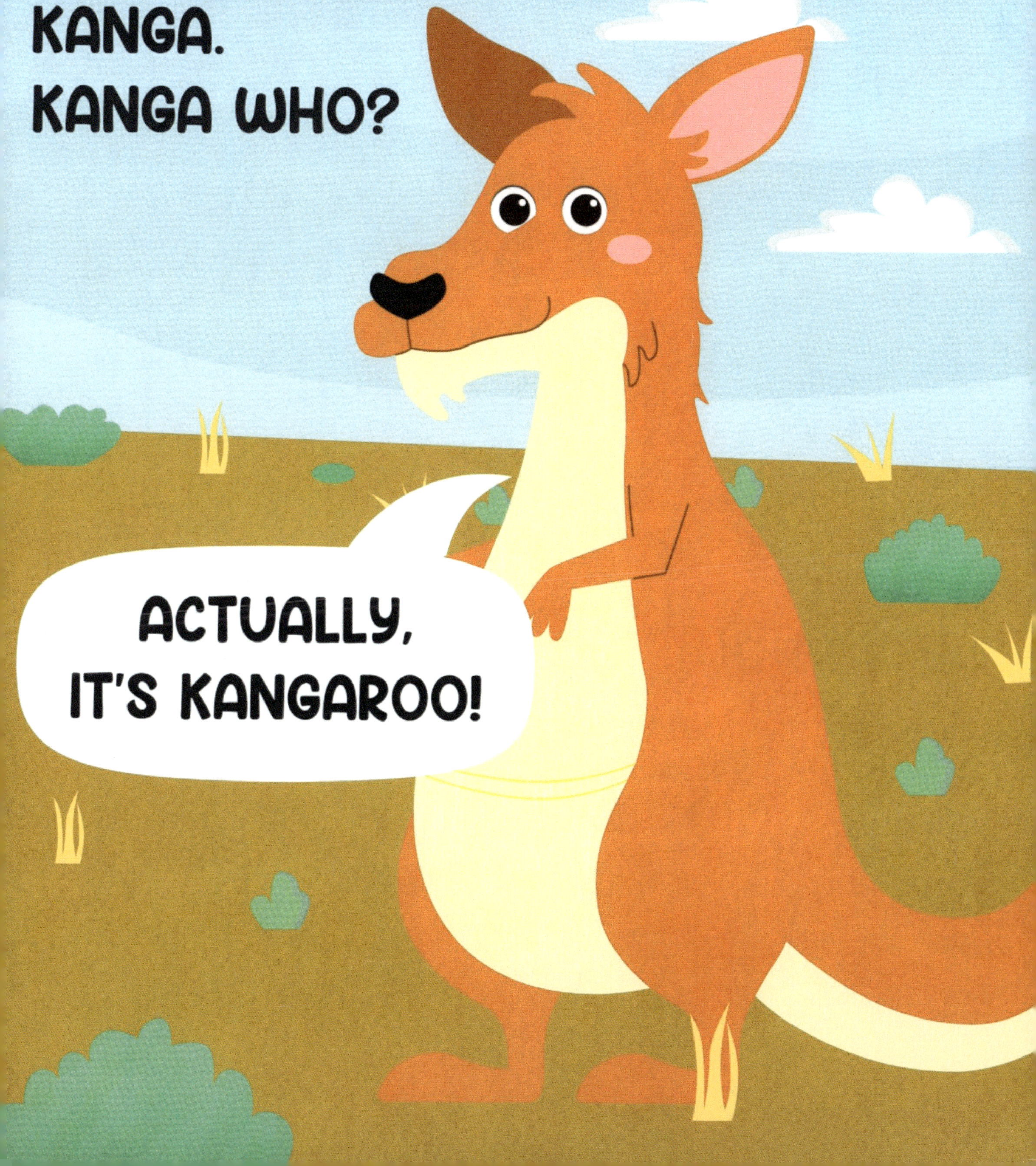

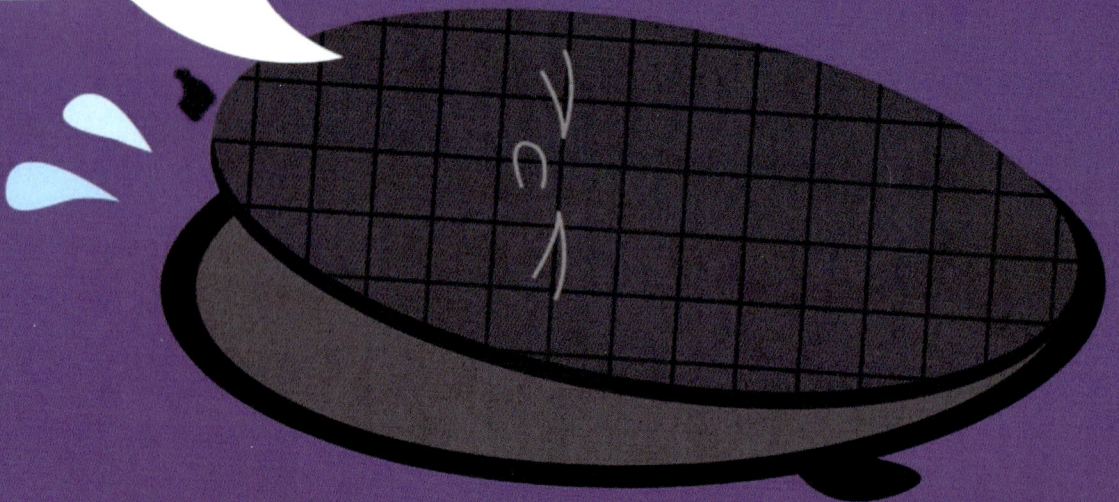

Read the tongue twisters as fast as you can!

I SCREAM, YOU SCREAM,
WE ALL SCREAM,
FOR ICE CREAM!

SHE SELLS SEA
SHELLS BY THE SEASHORE
AND THE SHELLS SHE SELLS
BY THE SEASHORE
ARE SEA SHELLS FOR SURE.

FUZZY WUZZY WAS A BEAR,
FUZZY WUZZY HAD NO HAIR,
FUZZY WUZZY WASN'T
VERY FUZZY, WAS HE?

HOW MUCH WOOD WOULD
A WOODCHUCK CHUCK, IF THE
WOODCHUCK COULD CHUCK WOOD?
HE WOULD CHUCK, HE WOULD,
AS MUCH AS HE COULD,
AND CHUCK AS MUCH WOOD
AS A WOODCHUCK WOULD

Amazon Book Review!

Our publishing team hopes you have enjoyed this book!

Would you take a minute to leave us a review on Amazon? It really helps us out! Thank you!

Scan the QR code below using the camera of your smartphone:

Manufactured by Amazon.ca
Bolton, ON